Be a Zillionaire

The Young Zillionaire's Guide to Producing Goods and Services

Juliana O. Tillema

rosen central

For my grandparents, Frances and Sherwood Moran.

Published in 2000 by The Rosen Publishing Group, Inc.
29 East 21st Street, New York, NY 10010

Copyright © 2000 by The Rosen Publishing Group, Inc.

First Edition

All rights reserved. No part of this book may be reproduced in any form without permission in writing from the publisher, except by a reviewer.

Library of Congress Cataloging-in-Publication Data

Tillema, Juliana O.
 The young zillionaire's guide to producing goods and services / Juliana O. Tillema.
  p. cm. — (Be a zillionaire)
 Includes bibliographical references and index.
 Summary: Provides information about producing goods and services using resource regulation, model economies, various means of predicting production, and private enterprise capitalism.
 ISBN 0-8239-3260-5
 1. Economics—Juvenile literature. 2. Production (Economic theory)—Juvenile literature. 3. Capitalism—Juvenile literature [1. Production (Economic theory) 2 Economics. 3. Capitalism.] I. Title. II. Series.
 HB183 .T55 2000
 338—dc21   00-021260

Manufactured in the United States of America

Table of Contents

1. Production ... What's That? — 4
2. Production Possibilities — 11
3. Everything Is a Trade-Off — 18
4. Economic Growth — 25
5. Trading Times — 32
6. Production ... Lemme Tell You All About It — 38

Glossary	40
For More Information	42
For Further Reading	45
Index	47

Production... What's That?

You hear the words "production," "productive," and "produce" all the time, right? But what do they mean? And what does this book have to do with those words? Let's look at how we use these words in our everyday lives and talk about what they mean. Then we will examine what production is from the point of view of an economist.

"I had a very productive summer selling cookies and lemonade at the park. I made more than $200."

"Let's go to the produce section of the grocery store and pick up some fresh fruit."

"Have you seen Rob Reiner's latest production, starring Michelle Pfeiffer and Bruce Willis?"

In each of these sentences, production indicates a commodity, which is something for sale. In the first sentence, cookies and lemonade were sold at the park. The person who made them earned summer spending money. In the second sentence, produce means fresh fruits and vegetables grown in the earth, harvested by workers, and shipped to a grocery store for you to buy and eat. In the last sentence, a production is a form of entertainment, in this case a movie, which you pay to watch.

Produce is a commodity.

Resource Regulation

Economists define production as the conversion of resources into goods and services. Goods are the cookies and lemonade, the fresh fruit, the movie, and other things for sale. Your blue jeans are goods. The resources that went into creating your jeans vary, depending on where you got them.

If your jeans came from the mall, the resources that went into their creation include the labor of the person operating the machine that sewed the zipper on the jeans and the sewing machine itself. The boat bound for the United States loaded with hundreds of thousands of pairs of jeans from China and the truck that transported the jeans to the mall are also resources used to produce your jeans.

If your aunt Sylvie made your jeans, the resources that went into their creation include the labor of the woman at the sewing store, who sold your aunt the denim she used for the jeans. Your aunt's time, her sewing machine, and her thread are also resources devoted to the production of your jeans.

Resources are generally divided into

Labor is one of the resources that created your jeans.

three categories: natural resources, human resources, and capital resources. Natural resources are water, land, air, and fire. The soil in which an apple tree grows to produce apples is a natural resource. The ocean across which your jeans sailed on a ship is also a natural resource. And the air that propels a windmill and causes it to generate power used to pump water or grind flour is also a natural resource.

Human resources are skills mined from humans. Human resources include physical labor, such as the labor involved in unloading a truck full of blue jeans or operating the machine that sews those jeans together. Human resources also include the intellectual labor of workers. The labor of the person writing this book is a human resource. The labor of the head of sales at the store where you bought your jeans is also a human resource. The job of the head of sales is to develop a plan to sell more blue jeans to more teenagers.

And finally, capital resources are the things that have been produced in order to aid in further production. An example of a capital resource is the sewing machine your aunt Sylvie or a laborer abroad used when sewing the jeans you wear.

Tasty Treats, Served Up Sweet

We already said that lemonade, apples, jeans, and movies are goods. In fact, economists categorize all of the things that people produce that have value as either goods or services.

Goods are tangible things, things you can touch or

eat or wash your hair with or wear. Capital goods are used to produce more goods, such as our trusty sewing machine, which produces jeans. Consumer goods are the jeans themselves.

The difference between the two types of goods is that capital goods are used to produce more goods, while consumer goods are the final products made for consumers to buy.

Services are actions that are performed by others. They are not tangible things. For example, a visit to the doctor, electricity in your home, a ride in a taxi, and table service in a restaurant are all services. You depend on other people to perform these actions and you pay those who perform them. If you are sick, you depend on the services of a doctor to heal you. In return for her services, you pay the doctor money. If you

Capital goods are used to produce more goods. Consumer goods are the products themselves.

A waiter in a restaurant is providing a service.

need to go to the airport, you pay for the services of a taxi driver to pick you up and get you there safely. We depend on electricity in our homes so that we can have light. Each month, your parents pay a fee to the electric company to keep the electricity on in your home—in doing so they are paying for a service.

Goods are commodities you buy to use. Services are actions performed by people who are paid.

Production Possibilities

2

We now know what production, resources, goods, and services are. We know that we consume things that are produced for many reasons—to make our lives easier, healthier, safer, and warmer. We know that some goods go into the production of more goods, while others fulfill our wishes and needs as consumers.

Endless Possibilities

Now that we understand what production is, let's discuss how much of something can be produced. There is a limit to how many pairs of jeans or stuffed animals or cookies can be produced. Many factors determine these limits—time, resources, demand, and more. But in order to understand our limits more clearly, we will build a model economy and follow a few, simple rules to help us understand how production works in the real world.

What Is a Model Economy?

A model economy is an economy that does not exist in the real world. It is an economy that we create and control in order to eliminate some of the complexity and some of the variables involved in economics. This will help us to understand the boundaries between what can and cannot be produced.

Our model economy will follow several rules. The first is that we will produce only two goods: carrots and cotton. The second rule is that everything we produce will be consumed in our economy. This means that we will never have extra cotton or carrots. It also means that our supply of capital resources, the things we use to create cotton and carrots—such as hoes and rakes and looms—will never grow or shrink. The third and final rule: You are the only person contributing to this economy.

The Production Possibility Frontier

In order to clothe yourself, you have to tend to the cotton plants, harvest the cotton at the appropriate time, and gather enough cotton to spin into cloth. After you use the loom to spin the cotton into cloth, you must cut the cloth and sew it into clothes that fit you. Obviously, making cloth is very time-consuming. In order to feed yourself, you must clear a patch in your garden, plant carrot seeds, hoe, water, and weed your garden, pull the carrots from the ground, and clean them. The maximum amount of time you can spend each day producing carrots and cotton is nine hours. If you work any more than this, you will quickly become exhausted!

In order to understand the limits of what can be produced in your model economy, we will draw a graph that explains a concept in economics called the production possibility frontier (PPF). This concept and graph define the limits of production in your model economy. The production possibility frontier is a fancy

The production possibility frontier defines the limits of what can be produced.

way of showing that you can produce different amounts of carrots and cotton in your model economy, and that there is a maximum amount of carrots and cotton beyond which you cannot produce.

There are different production possibilities in your model economy. For example, you could devote all of your time to growing carrots. After one month, this would result in there being no cotton for cloth and 50 pounds of carrots. Another possibility is producing only cotton and no carrots. But this would result in too much cotton and nothing to eat.

Another possibility: You could make 2 yards of cloth per month and produce 35 pounds of carrots per month. Still another possibility: You could produce 25 pounds of carrots and 3 yards of cloth. Let's pretend, given your size and appetite, that this is the perfect amount of cloth and carrots for you. It takes 3 yards of cloth to clothe you and 25 pounds

Production Possibility	Carrots (lbs./month)	Cloth (yds./month)
A	50	0
B	35	2
C	25	3
D	15	4
E	0	5

Production Possibility Frontier

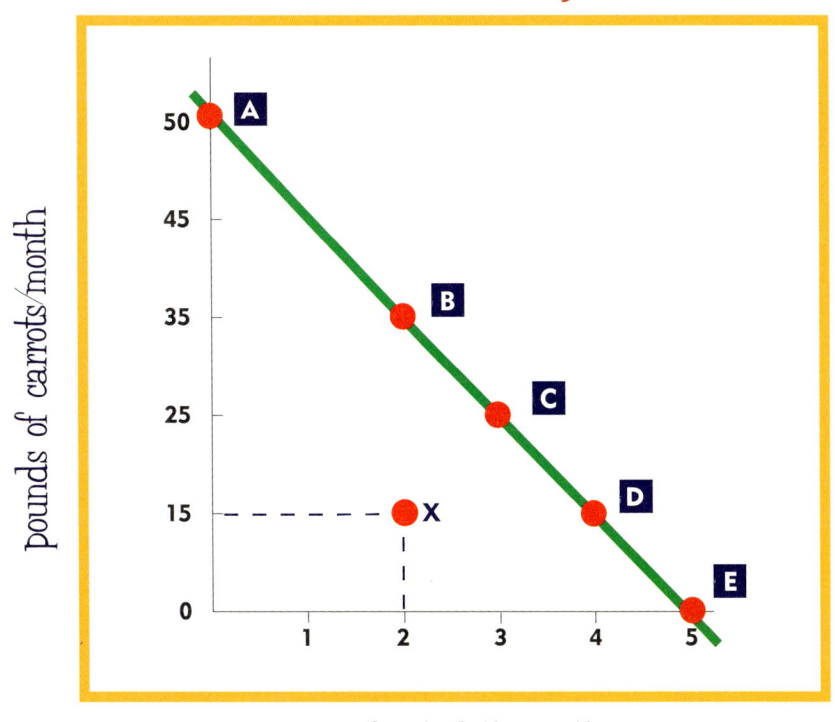

of carrots to keep you fed for one month. However, this does not mean that there are not other possibilities. You could also produce 15 pounds of carrots and 4 yards of cloth, or you could produce 5 yards of cloth and 0 pounds of carrots. The table above shows all five of these possibilities.

As you can see, there are many different possibilities. Only one is right for you. You need cloth to make clothes, and you need carrots to feed yourself.

In addition to the options listed above, you could also produce inside the production possibility frontier. You could produce 2 yards of cloth each month and 15 pounds of carrots (see point X on the graph). If you produce inside the production possibility frontier, you are not devoting the maximum amount of time and energy to production. If you did this, although you would still be producing carrots and cotton, you would be producing inefficiently. Perhaps you are devoting only five hours each day to producing carrots and cloth. It is possible and more efficient to produce more. This is what the production possibility frontier maps: the maximum amount you can produce if you work at your maximum capacity.

You cannot produce outside the production possibility frontier. It is not physically possible for you to work more than nine hours each day, nor is it possible for you to attain results greater than what you have been given to work with allows. You have been given some seeds for carrots, a hoe and rake, several acres of cotton plants, a loom and scissors and thread. You are limited by the technology you have been given. If you had a sewing machine, or a planting machine, or a harvesting machine, you could produce more carrots or cotton. Without these technological advancements, however, it is not physically possible to produce anything more than what we have mapped out on the graph on the previous page.

Do you notice a pattern to the chart and graph on the previous page? Do you see that the more carrots you produce, the less cotton you are able to produce? Similarly, the more cotton you produce, the fewer carrots you can produce.

In your model economy, you had to determine the best point for you to produce on the production possibility frontier. In order to do this, do you need to sit down and draw out the chart and graph? No. You do not need the graph of the production possibility frontier in order to figure out how much you need to eat and how much cloth you need.

You understand that some people eat more, whereas others eat less. You also know that some people are larger and require more cloth to cover their bodies. The production possibility frontier simply shows you all of your choices, even the choices that do not provide you with what you need for survival.

When you choose between one point and another, let's say between points B and D, you are confronted with the opportunity cost of your choices. Opportunity cost is the price you pay when you choose one thing over another. For example, in choice A, in order to have 50 pounds of carrots, you "pay" by having no cloth. Of course, paying a price does not refer to the money that you pay; rather, it refers to a choice that you make in which you forfeit one thing for another. In choice E, you pay for 5 yards of cloth by having no carrots. You can have 5 yards of cloth, but if you choose this option, you will have no food.

Everything Is a Trade-Off

In order to understand opportunity cost better, let's step back and examine the world on a larger level. Then let's zero in on financial choices you have to make in your own life.

Promises, Promises

When your governor was elected, what promises did she make to the voters? Did she say she would improve the schools? Did she promise to improve the benefits available for single parents?

These promises depend upon money. If the governor promises to improve schools by allocating more money to hire teachers, for better salaries, newer textbooks, or more computers, she must take money away from somewhere else. No one, not even politicians, has an unlimited supply of money.

Improving schools could mean cutting the money available to hire and train new police officers. Perhaps this is an ideal compromise. Perhaps you live in a state that has a relatively low crime rate, well-trained police officers, and no need right now to develop the police force further. If the governor promised to improve the benefits available to single parents, how might she do this? One way is to raise taxes. The additional money each person in the state pays on the property he or she owns will go toward providing child-care centers, health insurance, food stamps, and other assistance to single parents of small children.

When politicians make promises, they need money to take action.

I Want It All

Now, let's look at economics in your family. Let's say you've saved a part of your allowance each week over the summer and a part of the money you made selling cookies. You have saved $50 for new clothes for the fall and winter. If we return to the example of the blue jeans from the beginning of this book, you have two options: You can spend $30 at the store on a new pair of blue jeans, or your aunt Sylvie can make you a pair of jeans with cloth that costs $12.

If you choose the $30 jeans, your legs will look stylish, but you'll have only $20 for the rest of your wardrobe. If you choose the $12 jeans, maybe you won't look quite so stylish, and you certainly won't have a fancy label attached to your back-side. But you will have $38 left over for other pieces of clothing.

One final example of a trade-off: Let's say you want to watch a movie, eat popcorn, and still have money to buy a magazine, but you have only a $10 bill. If you go out to the movies and buy popcorn, you could easily spend almost all of the $10. You definitely

You have to make choices about how you spend your money.

Opportunity costs involve making decisions about what you are willing to give up in order to get something else that you want.

wouldn't have enough left over for the $3 magazine you wanted. But if you check out a movie from the library for free, and you make popcorn at home, you will still have enough money to buy the magazine.

Opportunity costs are all about what you are willing to give up in order to get something else that you want. Some people are willing to give up watching a movie on a big screen in order to purchase a magazine. Some people are not. Opportunity costs involve making decisions about what is best for you, in the case of the movies or the clothes; or what is best for a state, in the case of the promises the governor makes to the people.

Measuring Opportunity Cost

Let's return to our graph of the production possibility frontier (page 15) to examine opportunity costs in our model economy. We will measure how many yards of cloth you must give up in order to get more carrots, and how many pounds of carrots you must give up in order to get more cloth.

If you spend all of your time producing cloth, you will produce 5 yards of cloth and have no carrots. If you decide to give up 1 yard of cloth, and you produce only 4 yards of cloth, you will gain 15 pounds of carrots. This means that the opportunity cost of 15 pounds of carrots is 1 yard of cloth.

If you spend all of your time producing carrots, you will produce 50 pounds of carrots and no cloth. If you decide to give up 15 pounds of carrots, and you produce only 35 pounds of carrots, you will gain 2 yards of cloth. This means that the opportunity cost of 2 yards of cloth is 15 pounds of carrots.

Production Possibilities in the Real World

Let's leave our model economy behind and examine how opportunity cost might work in a factory in which we have more variables and a new product. Let's imagine you are in charge of a factory that makes stuffed animals. You have 10 employees, each of whom can make 100 stuffed animals each day. This means that your factory can make a total of 1,000 stuffed animals a day, 5 days a week.

To get the total number of stuffed animals your factory can produce each day, multiply the total number of employees—10—times 100 stuffed animals:

100x10 = 1,000 stuffed animals each day. How many stuffed animals can be produced in a 5-day workweek?

You have decided to have your workers make 2 types of stuffed animals: cows and pigs. You will have to make some choices, or trade-offs, in order to figure out how many of each type of stuffed animal you will produce.

If all 10 of your workers make pigs all day long, how many pigs will you have at the end of the day?

If 2 of your workers make cows all day, for a total of 200 cows, and the other 8 workers make pigs, for a total of 800 pigs, at the end of the day you will still have 1,000 total stuffed animals. However, 200 of them will be cows. You will be giving up 200 pigs in order to gain 200 cows.

If 5 of your workers make cows and 5 of your workers make pigs, how many stuffed animals will you have in total at the end of the day? How many pigs are you giving up to gain 500 cows?

This may seem confusing at first. Remember the lesson behind the math: For everything you choose to produce, you give up the possibility of producing as much of something else. You can produce one item or two items or three or ten or twenty, but the more you produce of one item, the less you will produce of another item. Just as you give up a movie on a big screen in order to have money to buy a magazine, you give up the possibility of producing 1,000 pigs if you assign 2 of your workers to make cows.

Economic Growth 4

In order to demonstrate what the production possibility frontier looks like, we created a model economy and examined a graph of the PPF. Then, we talked about trade-offs. However, we all know that the world around us is constantly changing. Sometimes we come up with a new idea that will make us more productive—such as using a sewing machine to sew clothes instead of doing it all by hand. Sometimes we are confronted with situations that make us less productive—it rains for seven days in a row, making it impossible for us to plant our garden.

Production possibilities are always changing. They may remain the same in our model economy, but in a real economy many factors change all of the time.

How do we describe expanding production possibilities? Economic growth is the term we use to describe expanding production possibilities. New technological developments and new ideas work together to help expand production possibilities.

Let's go back to our stuffed animal factory. If we keep all of the workers and all of the equipment we have, we will make 1,000 stuffed animals each day for many years. However, if we accumulate more capital resources, or tools, to help us in the production of more stuffed animals, we can make more than 1,000 stuffed animals each day. If we experience technological progress and develop new, better, and more efficient ways to produce stuffed animals,

Production possibilities are always changing.

we will also produce more than 1,000 stuffed animals. These are the two factors that allow economies to grow: capital resources and technological progress.

Unlimited Growth?

Can economies just grow and grow? Is there a price for economic growth? The answer is yes, of course there is a price for economic growth. Just as you must make decisions about how to spend your money, economies must make decisions that involve sacrificing something in the short term in order to gain long-term economic growth.

Capital resources and technological progress allow economies to grow.

In the stuffed animal factory, our production possibilities increase if we take 2 of the 10 stuffed animal makers off the production line and assign them to develop more tools. This means that only 8 workers will be making stuffed animals, for a total of 800 stuffed animals produced each day—200 stuffed animals less than we were making when all 10 of the workers were producing stuffed animals. We used to produce 1,000 stuffed animals each day. Now we produce 800 stuffed animals each day.

The 2 workers who used to produce 200 stuffed animals each day have now been assigned to develop faster sewing machines. These machines will allow each worker to make 150 stuffed animals each day. In the long run, the stuffed animal factory will produce more stuffed animals each week if it has advanced technological tools, in this case, faster sewing machines. The development of more advanced tools is called technological progress.

Let's say that the main stuffed animal boss has told you that you will be allowed to hire 5 more workers for the stuffed animal factory if you increase the total number of stuffed animals you produce. Once 2 of your workers have developed faster sewing machines, each of the other 8 workers will produce 150 stuffed animals each day for a total of 1,200 stuffed animals each day. Right?

- **8 workers x 150 stuffed animals each day = 1,200 stuffed animals total each day**

- **1,200 stuffed animals each day x 5 day workweeks = 6,000 stuffed animals total each workweek**

The other 2 workers will continue to develop technology and maintain the faster sewing machines.

Technological progress allows you to increase the number of resources you have in your factory. Your boss sees that your factory produces 1,200 stuffed animals each day and allows you to hire 5 new workers, 4 of whom will make stuffed animals, and 1 of whom will work to develop better tools for the factory. These workers are resources. You now have 12 workers producing stuffed animals, and 3 devoted to technological progress.

Technological progress allows you to increase your resources.

- **12 workers x 150 stuffed animals each day = 1,800 stuffed animals total each day**

Developing technologies is the opportunity cost of economic growth.

- **1,800 stuffed animals each day x 5 day workweeks = 9,000 stuffed animals total each workweek**

This is the story of economic growth. At first, you had to compromise the total amount your factory produced in order to devote extra workers to developing technology. After a short while, however, this technological progress paid off, and your factory was quickly able to produce more stuffed animals than it could before it implemented new technologies. The higher level of production led to an increase in resources, meaning that there were more workers and more people devoted to the development of technology. Your factory is a part of a growing economy.

The Cost of Change

What price do economies pay for growth? Economic growth means that there are a greater number of things to consume. For example, if we produce more stuffed animals, there are more toys available to us as consumers. If we produce more blue jeans, there are more blue jeans available to us as consumers. If an economy begins producing a greater number of many different things—more computers, more toys, more clothes, more sewing machines, does it experience unlimited growth?

The answer is no. Economic growth is not a guarantee that an economy will produce so many things that scarcity will disappear. As we saw earlier, we settle for less of one thing in order to get more of another. We have fewer workers in the stuffed animal factory in order to develop more tools. The more technological progress we experience, the more important it becomes to devote time and brain power to accumulating capital and developing technologies. Growth is not free. The opportunity cost of economic growth is producing fewer goods and devoting more time to developing technologies and resources.

Trading Times

Why do people trade? What benefits are involved in trade? Who trades, and what do they trade?

Wanna Trade Your Bologna Sandwich for My Tuna Fish?

In the lunchroom, you may trade sandwiches when you have a type of sandwich that you don't like. Hopefully you can find someone who wants what you have and who has something that you want. In our model economy, however, we have far fewer choices. In fact, all we have is enough to survive on. We don't have extras like bologna and tuna fish.

On your patch of earth in the model economy, you grow carrots for food and you harvest cotton for cloth. Let's say there is another person with a plot nearby, a girl named Junko. She grows corn to eat and tends sheep to get wool. Just like you, everything Junko produces, she consumes. Both you and Junko are self-sufficient.

Self-sufficiency describes the state in which everything that is produced is consumed. You are self-sufficient in your model economy. You use the cotton and the carrots you grow to clothe and feed yourself. In Junko's economy, she eats all of the corn that she produces and uses the wool to make warm clothes. There is nothing left over when you and Junko each produce at the most efficient points on your production possibility frontier.

You could try to produce wool and corn in your model economy. However, the soil in your plot is much better for growing carrots than corn, and there aren't any sheep where you live, either. This makes it very difficult for you to produce either corn or wool. Junko, on the other hand, has no experience growing carrots or harvesting cotton. She has never seen a cotton plant and doesn't know how deep to plant carrot seeds.

These differences lead to a comparative advantage. A person has a comparative advantage when he or she can produce goods at a lower cost than anyone else can. You could produce the goods that Junko produces, but it would be extremely difficult and it would take more time for you to produce wool and corn than for you to produce carrots and cotton. You would have to learn where to find sheep, how to look after them, and how to spin their wool.

Trading requires that you find someone who wants something you have and who has something that you want.

You would also have to learn how to plant and cultivate corn.

At this moment, however, you have a comparative advantage in the production of carrots and cotton. You know how to produce these things and you produce them with maximum efficiency. Junko, on the other hand, has a comparative advantage in the production of wool and corn. She knows how to produce these things with maximum efficiency.

If you and Junko are each self-sufficient, can you gain anything from trading with each other? Of course you can. You can have a greater variety of goods if you trade. If you continue to grow carrots and cotton, your opportunity cost will not change. You will produce the same amount of food and cloth that you did previously. Junko will also produce the same amount of food and cloth as she did before. However, if you trade, you will both have a surplus—you will have extra corn, carrots, woolen clothing, and cotton clothing. Junko will also have access to all of these products.

But How Does It Really Work?
In our model economy, there are only two people producing four goods. In the real world, there are millions of people producing many different products, few of which are exchanged directly using the barter system. In your model economy, you and Junko exchanged food and clothing using the barter system—you trade one good for another. In the lunchroom, you may also use the barter system, trading a sandwich that you don't really like for a yummier sandwich. A lunchroom trade requires that you find someone who is willing to trade with you; you must find someone who wants what you have. In the world economy, bartering may be less common than in the lunchroom. Because bartering is not relied upon in many economies, rules about property and money have been established to guide trade.

Property is anything of value. Land and buildings, ideas and music, books, houses, and equipment are all property. The clothes you are wearing and the pictures you

In the world economy, bartering is less common than in the lunchroom.

draw are your property. They belong to you and are valuable to you. In the United States, we follow laws stating that people own the things that they have made, as well as the things that they have purchased. People in the United States also own the things they have received by trading with others and the things that have been given to them as gifts.

The economic system found in the United States is called private enterprise capitalism. Private enterprise capitalism describes a system in which individuals are allowed to choose their economic activities and are permitted to own resources that may be used in production. This means that you may choose how and where you spend your money. You are also allowed to purchase things that will help you make more money.

If your aunt Sylvie wanted to make a living sewing clothes and selling them to people, she would need to purchase a second sewing machine, more fabric, thread, and patterns. If you wanted to make extra money in the summer by selling homemade cookies, you would need to purchase more chocolate chips and other ingredients, as well as a larger mixing bowl. This system, in which individuals may choose their economic activities and may own the tools they need to make money, is called private enterprise capitalism.

In an economic system such as this one, you may be able to see how trade could benefit you and those around you. You are skilled at making cookies, and you have the ingredients to make them. Your aunt is skilled at making clothing, and she has the equipment to make you a new outfit. If you each have an efficient means of producing a good that the other wants or needs, it is logical for you to trade with each other.

Show Me the Money

In our economic system, you are probably aware that we don't just trade with each other, but that we use money to buy the things that we want and need. Money is used in exchange for goods and services. We use money made and regulated by the government. We buy what has been produced by others with this money.

Production... Lemme Tell You All About It

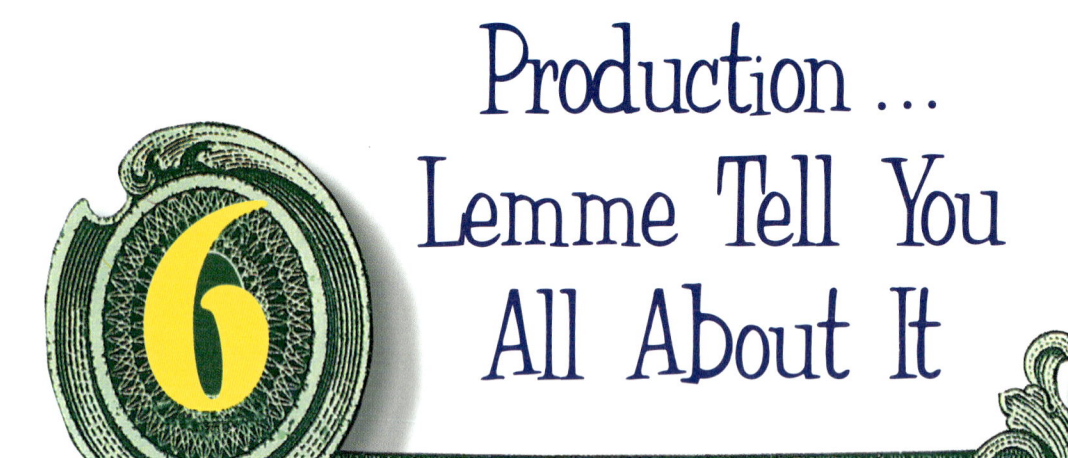

6

In this book, we have seen that production is the conversion of resources (such as your baking skills) into goods and services (such as cookies). We have built a model economy, in which you are self-sufficient and you consume all that you produce. We have come to understand production possibilities and have learned about the benefits of trading with our neighbor, Junko. We have discussed the costs of economic growth and the concept of private enterprise capitalism.

To conclude this book, I challenge you to see how the concepts we have discussed are relevant to your life. More specifically, what opportunity costs, or trade-offs, are you willing to make in your economic life, and what trade-offs are you unwilling to make? Where do you see examples of

Economics is about how we spend our money and resources.

economic growth in the world around you? Do you see economic growth in your school? How about technological progress? Do you know anyone who is economically self-sufficient? How is that person self-sufficient?

Although we created a model economy and drew graphs to demonstrate certain concepts about production, economics is much more complicated than models and graphs. Economics is about how we spend our money and resources; it's about who has money and resources and who does not, and why. Producing goods and services is one small piece of the economic pie. Try to answer one or two of the questions above, and apply some of the concepts discussed in this book to your life.

GLOSSARY

barter system System of trading one good for another good.

capital goods Resources that have been produced in order to help make more resources.

commodity Anything for sale.

comparative advantage The state in which a person or a group can produce something at a lower cost than anyone else.

consumer goods The final products, made to sell to the consumer.

economic growth The growth an economy experiences when its production possibilities expand.

goods Commodities you buy to use.

model economy An economy with only a few variables, unlike the real world economy.

opportunity cost What you are willing to give up in order to gain something else.

private enterprise capitalism The system whereby individuals may choose their economic activities and may own the tools they need to make money.

production The conversion of resources into goods and services.

production possibility frontier A concept that defines the limits of production.

property Anything of value that someone owns.

Glossary

resources Things used in the production of goods. Resources are generally divided into three categories: natural resources, human resources, and capital resources.

self-sufficiency The state in which everything that is produced is consumed.

services Actions you pay other people to perform.

technological progress New, more efficient ways to produce goods.

For More Information

Web Sites

Economic Education from the Federal Reserve Bank of San Francisco

This site provides curriculum materials, publications and resources, links for economics teachers, and links to other federal reserve sites dedicated to economic education.
Web site: http://www.frbsf.org/econedu/indx.eced.html

Economic Education from the Federal Reserve Bank of St. Louis

The goal of economic education at the Federal Reserve Bank of St. Louis is to support teachers in their instruction of how money, banking, and the Federal Reserve System work. It provides a variety of services and products designed for teachers.
Web site: http://www.stls.frb.org/education/econed1.html
Email: Dawn C. Griffitts, Economic Education Coordinator: dgriffitts@stls.frb.org
Telephone: (314) 444-8421
Fax: (314) 444-8503

Economics America

A nationwide, comprehensive program for economic education in America's schools that develops national and state content standards in economics, assists in development of national, state, and local standards-based curricula, publishes classroom-tested materials, provides university/college-based professional development for teachers, and conducts evaluations, assessment, and research.
Web site: http://www.economicsamerica.org

Econopolis

A Web site designed to make learning economics an interesting and fun process for children and their teachers. This site contains game boards, quizzes

For More Information

at the end of each lesson, links to other Internet sites, and a Teacher's Corner.
Web site: http://tqjunior.advanced.org/3901/index.htm

Government & Economics for Kids

A site that lets you visit the White House.
Web site: http://www.netforyou.net/kidszone/gov-ec.htm

The Journal of Economic Education

This journal offers original articles on innovations in and evaluations of teaching techniques, materials, and programs in economics.
Web site: http://www.indiana.edu/~econed

KIDLINK in the Economics Curriculum

This site provides descriptions and histories of currencies around the world, discusses children in the workplace and their wages, explains money in a math curriculum, and defines "needs" versus "wants."
Web site: http://www.kidlink.org/english/general/curric8.html

The National Association of Economic Educators

Roger Atwood, President-NAEE
Nebraska Council on Economic Education
339 College of Business Administration
University of Nebraska-Lincoln
Lincoln, NE 68588-0404
Telephone: (402) 472-2333

NAEE is the professional association of economic educators affiliated with the National Council on Economic Education. The goals of the NAEE are

For More Information

to encourage and support academically sound, objective, nonpartisan programs in economic education at all levels, and enhance communication and exchange of ideas among economic educators.

Web site: http://ecedweb.unomaha.edu/naee

National Council on Economic Education

A unique nonprofit partnership of leaders in education, business, and labor devoted to helping youngsters learn to think, to choose, and to function in a changing global economy.

Web site: http://www.nationalcouncil.org

Other Web Sites of Interest:

Kidsense—sponsored by John Nuveen & Company
www.kidsenseonline.com

Young Investors Network—sponsored by Salomon Smith Barney
www.smithbarney.com/yin

For Further Reading

Bangs, David H., and Linda Pinson. *The Real World Entrepreneur Field Guide*. New York: Upstart Press, 1999.

Bendick, Jeanne, and Robert Bendick, *Markets: From Barter to Bar Codes*. Danbury, CT: Franklin Watts, 1997.

Burkett, Larry, and Todd Temple. *Money Matters for Teens Workbook*. Chicago, IL: Moody Press, 1998.

Giesbrecht, Martin Gerhard, and Gary E. Clayton. *A Guide to Everyday Economic Thinking*. New York: McGraw-Hill, 1997.

Giulio, Maestro, et al. *The Story of Money*. San Angelo, TX: Mulberry Avenue Books, 1995.

Godfrey, Neale S., and Randy Verougstraete. *Neale S. Godfrey's Ultimate Kids' Money Book*. New York: Simon & Schuster, 1998.

Heilbroner, Robert, and Lester Thurow. *Economics Explained*. New York: Simon & Schuster, 1994.

Karnes, Frances A., et al. *Girls and Young Women Entrepreneurs: True Stories About Starting and Running a Business Plus How You Can Do It Yourself*. Minneapolis, MN: Free Spirit, 1997.

Mariotti, Steve (with Tony Towle and Debra DeSalvo). *The Young Entrepreneur's Guide to Starting and Running a Small Business*. New York: Times/Random House, 1999.

For Further Reading

Otfinoski, Steven. *The Kid's Guide to Money: Earning It, Saving It, Spending It, Growing It, Sharing It.* New York: Scholastic, 1996.

Roper, Ingrid. *Moneymakers: Good Cents for Girls.* Middleton, WI: Pleasant Company Publications, 1998.

Sweidt, Maryann N. *Mr. Blue Jeans: A Story About Levi Strauss.* Minneapolis, MN: First Avenue Editions, 1992.

Index

B

bartering/trading, 32–37, 38

C

capital resources, 7, 12, 26, 27

comparative advantage, 33, 34

D

demand, 11

E

economic growth, 26, 27, 30, 31, 38, 39

G

goods, 5, 7, 8, 10, 11, 12, 31, 33, 34, 35, 37–39

M

model economy, 12–17, 22, 32–35, 38–39

money, 5, 10, 17, 18–21, 27, 35, 37, 39

O

opportunity cost, 17, 18, 21–22, 31, 35, 38

P

production possibilities, 14, 22–24, 25–26, 28, 38

production possibility frontier, 12–17, 22, 25

R

resources, 5–7, 11, 29–31, 36, 38, 39

S

self-sufficiency, 33, 34, 38, 39

services, 5, 7, 8–10 11, 37, 38, 39

T

technological developments/progress, 16, 26–27, 28–31, 39

time, 6, 11, 16, 22, 31, 33

CREDITS

About the Author
Juliana O. Tillema lives and writes in Brooklyn, New York.

Photo Credits
Cover photo's © Artville; p. 5, 30 © Image Bank; p. 6 © Beele Caerney/UniPhoto; p. 8 © Reuters/David Loh/Archive Photos; p. 9 © Bob Daemmrich/UniPhoto; pp. 13, 27 © SuperStock; p. 19 © Reuters/Remy Steinegger/Archive Photos; p. 20 by Thaddeus Harden; pp. 21, 34, 36, 39 by Maura Boruchow; p. 26 © UniPhoto; p. 29 © Gordon M. Kurzweil/UniPhoto.

Series Design
Law Alsobrook

Layout
Laura Murawski